POINT OF IMPACT

The Invention of the Silicon Chip

A Revolution in Daily Life

WINDSOR CHORLTON

Heinemann Library
Chicago, Illinois

Produced for Heinemann Library by Discovery Books Limited
Designed by Sabine Beaupré
Originated by Ambassador Litho Limited
Printed in Hong Kong

06 05 04 03 02
10 9 8 7 6 5 4 3 2 1

Library of Congress Cataloging-in-Publication Data
Chorlton, Windsor.
  The invention of the silicon chip : a revolution in daily life /
Windsor Chorlton.
      p. cm. -- (Point of impact)
Includes bibliographical references and index.
Summary: Examines the events surrounding the development of the silicon chip, its uses, and its impact on civilization.
  ISBN 1-58810-554-7 (lib. bdg.)   ISBN 1-4034-0073-3 (pbk. bdg.)
  1. Integrated circuits--History--Juvenile literature. 2.
Semiconductor wafers--History--Juvenile literature. 3.
Microelectronics--Social aspects--Juvenile literature. [1. Integrated
circuits--History. 2. Microelectronics--Social aspects.] I. Title. II.
Series.
  TK7820 .C54 2002
  621.3815--dc21
                              2001003478

Acknowledgments
The author and publishers are grateful to the following for permission to reproduce copyright material:
Corbis, pp. 4, 5, 6, 8, 9, 10, 12, 13, 14, 15, 17, 20, 21, 24, 26, 28, 29; Hulton Getty, pp. 7, 11; Safeway, p. 16; Devendra Shrikhande/Discovery Photo Library, pp. 18, 23; BBC Worldwide, p. 19; NASA, p. 23; NOAA/National Weather Service, p. 25; Volvo Cars of North America, p. 27.

Cover photographs reproduced with permission of: (top) easyEverything; (bottom) Corbis.

Every effort has been made to contact copyright holders of any material reproduced in this book. Any omissions will be rectified in subsequent printings if notice is given to the publisher.

Some words are shown in bold, **like this.** You can find out what they mean by looking in the glossary.

Contents

Kilby's Idea

A new type of circuit

In July 1958, the Texas Instruments **electronics** plant in Dallas, Texas, closed for an annual holiday. The only engineer left at work was Jack Kilby, who had joined the company two months earlier and was not entitled to take time off. Kilby had been hired to develop a new type of **electrical circuit.** He was not happy with the proposed design because he thought it was too big and expensive.

Alone in his laboratory, Kilby tried to come up with a better design. He read and thought and sketched. Suddenly the answer came to him. Instead of making the circuit out of lots of separate parts, why not make the whole thing out of a single piece of **silicon**? Within two months, Kilby had a working model: a complete electrical circuit only half an inch (one centimeter) long. Texas Instruments called it the "solid circuit." Today, it is better known as the integrated circuit, the microchip, or the silicon chip.

Silicon chips are usually smaller than 2 in. (5 cm) on each side. Sometimes they are no more than a millimeter. Silicon chips consist of hundreds, even millions, of parts made from one piece of silicon.

Before the invention of the silicon chip, there were only a few computers. The first general-purpose computer, called the Electronic Numerical Integrator and Calculator (ENIAC), weighed 33 tons and used enough electricity to power 15 large homes. Despite this, it still had less computing power than an average laptop today.

The beginning of a revolution

Kilby thought his invention would make radios and televisions smaller and cheaper. He never imagined that it would transform room-sized computers into today's laptops or lead to many other inventions, from mobile telephones and bar code scanners to video games and the Internet.

Chips for many purposes

The fifteen billion chips now in existence are the building blocks of our age. They control labor-saving devices such as **robots** and photocopiers. They enable telephone systems to handle millions of calls at one time. Installed in machines such as electron microscopes or **satellite** cameras, they reveal new information about our world and beyond. As the "brains" in computers, silicon chips can store and exchange massive amounts of information.

INVENTING THE FUTURE

In 1998, 40 years after Kilby invented the silicon chip, Tom Engibous, chairman of Texas Instruments, said, "*Jack* [Kilby] *did more than invent the integrated circuit that day—he invented the future.*"

Home Life Before the Chip

The age of change

The 1950s were a time of rapid change. Jet airplanes were crossing the Atlantic Ocean, and the first **satellites** were put into orbit around Earth. Yet people still listened to music by playing records on scratchy-sounding gramophones, as they had done 50 years before. Children often played with homemade wooden toys, as their grandparents had done.

Television viewers in the 1950s had fewer choices than they have today. Early shows were all in black and white. Although there were color televisions by the 1950s, few people could afford to buy them.

Radio and television

In the 1950s, people relied on the radio more than they do today for news and their favorite programs. For many, television was the **electronic** marvel of the age. By 1959, television sets in the home were common, and watching television became a popular leisure activity.

Appliances such as radios and televisions in the 1950s used **vacuum tubes.** The tubes acted as **valves** to make electrical current flow in the right direction. They were also **amplifiers** that increased the current's strength. However, vacuum tubes were fragile, used a lot of power, and got very hot. In those days, radios and televisions were as large as pieces of furniture because vacuum tubes took up a lot of space. Televisions were expensive, took a long time to start up when they were turned on, and had poor sound and picture quality. Most of all, like many appliances of the time, they often broke down completely.

Domestic appliances

Televisions became more affordable as the 1950s progressed, as did other electrical appliances, but they were still considered luxury items. Dishwashers were unusual, and washing machines were simple machines with no electronic parts. Many people still washed their laundry by hand. There were fewer labor-saving devices in the kitchen to chop, mix, and prepare foods.

Before the **silicon** chip, people spent more time on domestic chores. Most women with families worked at home rather than going out to work.

Out and About

School and work

At school in the 1950s, there were no videos or computers, and so all information was printed in schoolbooks. All work was written by hand, and there were no calculators to help in math classes. Instead, children used **slide rules** and printed tables to help them with their calculations.

In the 1950s, many students finished school at the age of sixteen and went to work. Most men still worked in manual jobs in the 1950s. In the country, this could be farmwork, but most people lived in cities or towns. Many worked in factories.

Women who worked outside the home often had jobs in shops or as typists, clerks, or secretaries. Office workers spent a lot of time filing papers and copying documents by hand or on typewriters. There were no computers to correct typing mistakes: work just had be done again from the beginning until it was right.

Before computers kept them indoors, children in the 1950s spent more of their free time playing outside than they do today. Playing in the street was safer because there were fewer cars on the road. These children are cooling themselves in the spray of a fire hydrant during a heatwave in 1959.

Traveling and communication

In 1950 there were only a few cars on the road compared to today. Many more people made their daily journeys on trains and buses than they do now. Cars were expensive because they were largely assembled by hand. They were also much simpler, with few **electronic** parts. So, although cars broke down a lot, they were fairly easy to repair because they didn't contain a lot of complicated equipment.

In the 1950s, making a phone call, even to someone in the same town, might require an operator to connect the call. It could take several minutes for a connection to be made. Quite often, callers could not get through at all. Long-distance calls were much more expensive than today, so they were made only on important occasions. Most long-distance communication was by done by mail. If it was urgent, people sent telegrams—messages sent along wires using electrical **signals.** The messages were then written out and delivered by a post office messenger.

Workers inspect and test typewriters in an office equipment factory in the 1950s. Before the **silicon** chip, factories relied more on people to run the machinery and to assemble parts by hand.

GOING SHOPPING

Most people shopped at small, local stores. People usually walked to the shops in their neighborhood, unless they lived in the country. Supermarkets were not common, and they were not nearly as big as they are now. Before the silicon chip, shopkeepers had to keep track of their stock and do their ordering by making lists of what they had. The only way to do this was to count every item on the shelves.

The First Step

Replacing the vacuum tube

The **vacuum tubes** in early **appliances** were large and unreliable. So scientists worked to find better ways of controlling **electronic** equipment. At Bell Telephone Laboratories in New Jersey, researchers tried making miniature replacements for vacuum tubes out of **silicon** and **germanium.** The researchers found that they could control the way electric current flowed through silicon and germanium by coating them with certain chemicals.

John Bardeen, William Shockley, and Walter Brattain (left to right) are pictured here at Bell Laboratories in 1948. They won the Nobel Prize in 1956 for their invention of the transistor.

The invention of the transistor

Scientists Walter Brattain and John Bardeen made a breakthrough in December 1947. They applied an electric current to gold wires on a plastic triangle held over a crystal of germanium. They found that the germanium **amplified** the **signal,** making it nearly 100 times stronger. This device came to be called a **transistor.** Transistors, like vacuum tubes, could control electric current, but they were more reliable and used less power.

A few weeks after Brattain and Bardeen's discovery, their colleague William Shockley designed a more efficient type of transistor that consisted of three layers of germanium sandwiched together.

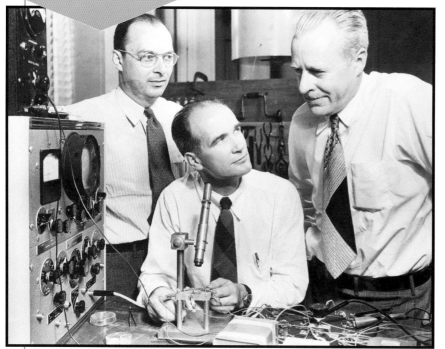

These transistors were so small that the entire **electrical circuit** of a radio could fit into the space taken up by a single vacuum tube. After 1960, transistors were made of silicon, which is cheaper than germanium and works better at high temperatures.

Transistors catch on

Transistors were soon put to greater use. They made telephone calls more efficient, and the first hearing aids using transistors were produced in 1952. Likewise, the U.S. military now had smaller, more reliable electronic parts for its computers and **guided missiles.**

Transistor radios first appeared in 1954. This picture from the 1950s shows how small they were compared to radios that used vacuum tubes. Transistor radios were popular with young people because they were small and cheap. Soon, radio stations began playing popular music for this audience.

WHAT IS SILICON?

Silicon is a very common **element** found in minerals such as quartz and sand. Silicon and germanium are called semiconductors because they are neither pure **conductors,** like metals, nor pure **insulators,** like rubber. On a piece of silicon, one area can be chemically treated to conduct electricity, while another area can be treated to prevent the flow of electricity.

Chips and Wafers

Trouble with transistors

Early **transistors** were not perfect. They had to be made by hand, and technicians had to look through microscopes to attach tiny wires. A speck of dirt could ruin a transistor. In any batch made, it was lucky if more than half worked properly.

The unreliability of transistors worried the military. They found that many of their multi-million-dollar **guided missiles** failed because of faulty transistors worth only a few dollars each. And although early transistors were much smaller than **vacuum tubes,** the transistorized missile-guidance systems still took up a lot of space.

The silicon chip

The chip that Jack Kilby invented in 1958 solved the problems of transistors and did much more. This miniature marvel contained tiny transistors and all the other parts of an **electrical circuit** on a piece of **silicon** no bigger than a thumbnail. The only drawback was that it was difficult and expensive to make.

Here, Jack Kilby is surrounded by some of the devices that have resulted from the invention of the silicon chip.

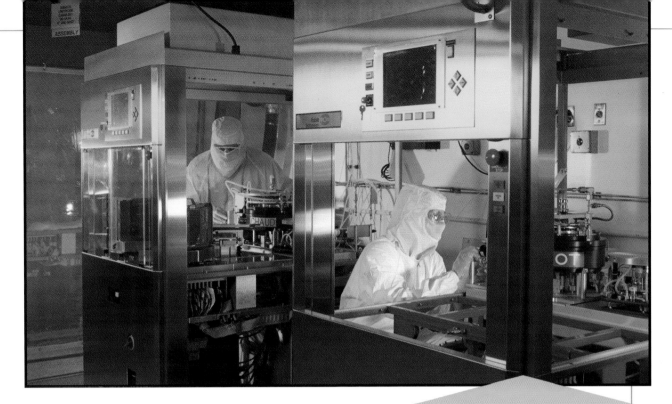

Noyce's wafers

However, Kilby wasn't the only engineer working on the problem. In 1959, at Fairchild Semiconductor in California, Robert Noyce developed a silicon chip built up in thin slices, called wafers, that could hold even more transistors in a tiny space. Kilby was awarded the Nobel Prize for his invention, but it was Noyce's design for a miniature electrical circuit that went into **mass production.**

Even the tiniest speck of dust can spoil a delicate silicon chip, so chips are made in spotless areas known as "clean rooms." A pattern is made on the silicon chip to form a circuit of transistors and other parts. Tiny pieces of aluminum are then added to connect the circuit together.

HOW SILICON CHIPS WORK

Like the nerve cells in our bodies, silicon chips control all of the other parts. When current is applied to the circuit on a chip, the chip will direct an **electronic** device. The transistors and other parts on the chip act as **valves** and pumps, guiding the flow of the electrical current. By arranging the same parts in different ways, chips can be **programmed** to control the performance of a huge range of devices, from computers and **digital** cameras to **robots** and TV remote controls. Many devices can be linked to make a complex system, such as a telephone network or an air traffic control system.

Rockets and Calculators

Chips in space

The immediate effect of the **silicon** chip was hard to see in business and daily life. When silicon chips first went on sale in 1961, they cost hundreds of dollars each. Most manufacturers went on using old-fashioned **transistors.** Early chips were used mainly in **guided missiles** and spacecraft.

Costly calculators

Texas Instruments was very worried about the poor sales of its silicon chips. The company asked Jack Kilby to design a portable calculator just to show the benefits of miniature chip **technology.** Existing transistorized calculators weighed 55 pounds (25 kg).

The model that Kilby produced in 1967 could fit into a coat pocket, but it cost hundreds of dollars. Gradually, as more chips were made and they got cheaper, so did calculators.

It is hard to believe that there were **satellites** in space before there were pocket calculators. In 1958, these army scientists launched America's first satellite. Amazingly, they were using a **slide rule** (seen lying to the left on the desk) to make their calculations during the countdown.

Quartz watches were among the few products that did use silicon chips in the early days. The first quartz watches were expensive, but now they are so inexpensive that businesses give them away as gifts.

No future for computers

The computer industry was the other main market for silicon chips, but even though chips made it possible to build computers a fraction of the size of earlier models, nobody thought there would be a demand for computers in the home or office.

In 1971, Intel, a company cofounded by Robert Noyce, worked out how to put the operating parts of a computer on a single silicon chip. Using this **microprocessor,** it became possible to build computers small enough to fit on a desk. Even then, the big manufacturers did not believe that the general public would buy computers. Instead, microprocessors were used in household items such as televisions and microwave ovens to make them run more efficiently.

MULTIPLYING TRANSISTORS

Scientists are always working on making silicon chips more powerful. The number of transistors that can be placed on a silicon chip doubles about every eighteen months. The most advanced chips today contain 30 million transistors.

The Apollo spacecraft that landed the first men on the moon in 1969 was guided by an onboard computer containing 5,000 silicon chips. By the time of the last Apollo mission in 1975, a pocket calculator carried by one of the astronauts had more processing power than the 1969 computer.

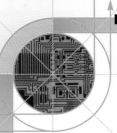

The Information Revolution Begins

Information in bar codes

One of the biggest changes brought about by the **silicon** chip was the new ability of machines to process information. Chip-controlled scanners in

computers, registers, and other machines read bar codes—patterns of stripes that contain information. On June 26, 1974, the first bar code scanner was used at a supermarket in Troy, Ohio. The first item scanned was a pack of chewing gum. From then on, bar codes and scanners appeared everywhere.

Today, nearly everything you buy has a bar code on it. The bar code for this book is shown above. Most stores have a scanner system that reads prices from bar codes. At the supermarket pictured here, groceries are passed over the scanner panel in front of the cashier.

Bar codes can show prices or the quantity of an item in stock. They can also track parcels and letters all over the world. Bar codes are used to identify patients in hospitals, and scientists have even put bar codes on insects to monitor their behavior.

The first desktop computers

Computers that fit on top of a desk, called personal computers or PCs, appeared in 1975. The first ones were sold as kits to be assembled by the buyer. In 1976, Steve Jobs and Steve Wozniak started selling a preassembled computer, "Apple I," which they built in a garage in Silicon Valley, California. It was a few years, though, before big business took notice.

IBM, the largest maker of business machines, finally realized that small computers could be useful. In 1981, IBM launched the IBM-PC for office use.

Computers join the workforce

Many people did not like the new **technology** at first. They worried about losing information if they pressed the wrong key. Some managers, used to having secretaries type their paperwork, resented having to learn to use a computer. The benefits of personal computers soon became obvious, though. With computers, it was possible to correct spelling mistakes and move text around without retyping. Most importantly, information stored and processed in computers could be found or used at the touch of a button.

Silicon Valley in California has been the base of the computer industry since the invention of the silicon chip. In the 1990s, when this picture was taken, it also became the headquarters of many hundreds of new businesses that sprang up when the Internet boom began.

SILICON VALLEY

Until the 1960s, the area between San Francisco and San Jose, California, was mainly a fruit-growing region. After Noyce's invention of the silicon wafer chip, the first silicon chips were **mass-produced** there. The name "Silicon Valley" was first applied to the area in 1971. Today, the valley is home to more than 3,000 high-tech companies, including Intel, Sun Microsystems, Oracle, and Silicon Graphics.

Entertaining Chips

Computers at home

Soon, people began buying computers for home use. They used them for writing letters, keeping family budgets, and playing games. Beginning in the mid-1980s, computer sales soared. Less than twenty years after the big manufacturers had insisted that nobody would want a personal computer, people were finding that they could not live without them.

Today, people use computers at home to produce all kinds of things that would have required a professional printer before. People make their own posters and leaflets, illustrate reports, and even publish magazines.

The 1980s saw the arrival of small, portable video games that could be used anywhere. New electronic games and toys appear in stores every year. These handheld units are relatively inexpensive and offer over 250 different games.

Video games

In 1972, American computer scientist Nolan Bushnell invented a simple bat-and-ball game that could be played on machines in restaurants and arcades. Bushnell called it "Pong," after the sound made when a player hit the ball. The first machine was installed in a bar in California. The constant "pong" noise began to attract curiosity. The next morning, people were lining up to play the new game.

The computer and video game craze had started. Within a few years, the **electronic** beeps of computer games would become a familiar sound all around the world.

The television generation

The changes in television since the **silicon** chip have been dramatic. **Digital** images create sharp pictures, and advances in manufacturing have produced reliable, inexpensive television sets. Homes around the world can receive hundreds of channels beamed by **satellites** from other countries.

Special effects and **animation** on television and in movies have greatly improved. In the 1939 film *The Wizard of Oz*, a tornado was simulated by someone twirling a piece of fabric. In the 1996 blockbuster *Twister*, the scenes of tornadoes hurling trucks through the air were created using computers.

Stunning special effects are created with the help of silicon chips. In 2000, a television documentary about dinosaurs used computer animation to create images that seemed as if they had been filmed in real life.

THE DIGITAL AGE

In digital equipment, silicon chips convert **signals** of any kind—such as musical notes, words, or pictures—into numbers and then convert them back into their original form. This process eliminates any bad quality in the signal, which explains why digital sound recordings, such as those on compact discs, are clearer than non-digital ones, such as those on old vinyl records.

Working with New Technology

Changes in the workplace

Although it took many years for the **silicon** chip to find its way into the workplace, there is no question that it has had a great impact. The kind of work people do and how they do it has changed dramatically.

Robots have taken over many manual jobs such as welding, paint spraying, and inspecting parts for faults. They can perform the same task perfectly over and over again. Cars, such as the ones being made in this factory, can be produced much more cheaply and much faster than before the silicon chip.

Tools and **technology** that we take for granted, and that make our jobs easier and faster, just did not exist twenty years ago.

Chips take over old jobs

Computers are used at every stage of the business process. People use them to design offices, factories, and new products. Silicon chips control the movement of products from the factory to the places where they are sold. Above all, chips control the machines that perform manual tasks in factories.

ROBOTS AT WORK

The first factory robots appeared in 1961. As robots get more "intelligent," they are used to replace people in more and more jobs and to bring additional skills to many areas of work. This use of robots does not mean fewer jobs for people. As robots and technology make businesses more efficient, the companies can grow and employ more people.

Chips create new jobs

Because of factory **robots,** there are fewer manual manufacturing jobs, and more people work in offices than ever before. Silicon chip technology has greatly reduced the amount of time office workers spend on routine tasks such as filing and copying. Information that would have taken people days to process before the silicon chip is now processed by a computer in minutes, and yet new jobs are being created all the time. Computer **programming,** providing services to high-technology businesses, and working with new forms of mass media are some of the jobs of the "computer age."

Some robots are used to carry out dirty or dangerous tasks such as investigating suspected bombs or moving nuclear waste. The robot shown here is picking up a piece of decorative glass from the shipwrecked *Titanic*. The ship sank in 1912, and years passed before new technology made it possible to recover some of its remains.

The Shrinking World

Getting connected

Another huge change brought about by **silicon** chip **technology** is in communications. There have been many improvements in the last 40 years. It is now much easier and faster to make contact with people in different parts of the world.

In the 1950s, making an international telephone call was complicated, and a letter could take weeks to get from one country to another. Now, because telephone systems use silicon chips, millions of calls are made every day cheaply and efficiently. Telephone lines are also used for quickly sending documents on fax machines. Chips also control **satellites** and mobile telephones. With a mobile satellite phone, which sends **signals** via a satellite high above the Earth, you could call home even from the top of Mount Everest.

Satellites do a lot more than just send telephone signals. As they circle Earth, they receive and transmit television shows from one part of the world to another, and they also send back pictures from space.

The Internet

The Internet would not exist without silicon chips. Based on an American military computer network, the Internet started in the late 1960s. Today, any computer user with a **modem** and telephone can use the Internet. Once "online," people instantly can send **electronic** mail—more commonly called e-mail—to other Internet users anywhere in the world. They can also look through masses of information on the thousands of websites that make up the World Wide Web. People use the Internet to do research, read the latest news, listen to music, watch videos, and shop.

No need to travel

Because of all of these developments in communication, there are more and more links between people and businesses in different countries. Workers thousands of miles apart can "teleconference," using computers and video cameras to discuss ideas or show new products without leaving their offices.

Chip technology gives people the ability to go shopping anywhere in the world without leaving their homes. Internet websites offer a range of goods not found in any one city or country, and with a credit card, shoppers can pay in any currency because computers automatically convert the payment.

Helping to Make Life Better

Here you can see a patient entering a machine tube for an MRI (magnetic resonance imaging) scan. The computer monitor in front shows a cross-section of the patient's body as she moves through the scanner, creating a picture that can be used to detect problems inside the body.

Medical breakthroughs

Many people live healthier and better-quality lives thanks to **silicon** chips. Computerized life-support systems monitor the condition of patients in intensive care units. Scanners controlled by chips can show detailed images of babies inside their mothers and help doctors detect any problems. If a patient with a rare type of blood needs a blood transfusion, computer **databases** enable doctors to find quickly the right type of blood anywhere in the country.

Three-dimensional computer **animation** is used to train surgeons in tricky operations where a slip

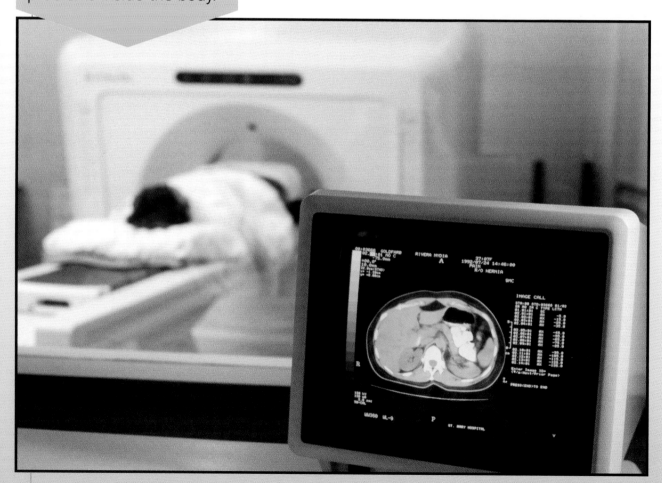

of the hand could harm the patient. In the operating room, some types of surgical equipment are guided by **robots,** which do not suffer from unsteady hands.

Overcoming disabilities

People with heart conditions can be fitted with pacemakers. These little devices are controlled by tiny chips and keep human hearts going in a nearly natural manner. Silicon chips implanted in the ear help deaf people hear. Blind people can "read" with the help of a computerized machine. The device scans printed pages and converts the information into a **digital** form that is then translated into spoken words.

Watching the weather

Knowing what the weather will do is important. In parts of the world threatened by tornadoes or flooding, accurate forecasts can save lives. Supercomputers, which work hundreds of thousands of times faster than personal computers, have greatly improved weather forecasts because they analyze information and make predictions quickly and accurately. Fifty years ago, weather forecasts were wrong as often as they were right. Today, weather forecasters get it right nine times out of ten and can give reasonably accurate forecasts for up to five days ahead.

These weather forecasters are issuing warnings from the weather center in Norman, Oklahoma, during a severe tornado outbreak in May 1999. With the help of their equipment and computers, they were able to issue warnings to areas where the tornadoes were likely to strike. The warnings saved hundreds of lives.

Chips in Daily Life

Around the home

If you look at the various electrical devices in your home, you would probably find that they are all regulated by **silicon** chips. Ovens, microwaves, dishwashers, and washing machines have all become cheaper to produce and more reliable to use. Because of this, many more people now own labor-saving devices. Household chores take up much less of our time now.

As more and more schools purchase computers and connect to the Internet, students have growing access to information from around the world.

Chips in the classroom

Chip **technology** has opened up a new world of learning. The contents of a large, expensive set of encyclopedias costing hundreds of dollars can now fit on an inexpensive CD-ROM. **Animation** and sound can be added, and the tiny package becomes a huge reference source on a classroom computer. Most schools use chip technology for everything from their science equipment to their communication systems.

Chips on the road

The use of computers and **robots** in factories has made cars more affordable and dependable, and the vehicles themselves use more and more silicon chip technology to operate. The onboard computers fitted to many new cars monitor how much fuel they use and if they are giving off polluting fumes. Some dashboard displays let the driver know when their car needs servicing, or even if a tire needs more air in it.

CHIPS IN EVERYTHING

Silicon chips have found their way into the most unlikely places. You can send greeting cards with more computing power than was used in the first spacecraft. Tiny chips embedded under the skin of cats and dogs make it possible to identify pets and return them to their owners if they get lost.

This navigation system on a car dashboard can be **programmed** to help drivers find their way. The driver enters his or her destination and location, and the car's computer maps a route for the driver to follow. Some cars now have a global positioning system that uses **satellite signals** to show drivers exactly where they are.

The Revolution Continues

How new inventions change lives

All important inventions cause **revolutions.** The invention of the steam engine 200 years ago sped up transportation and made **mass-produced** goods affordable for ordinary people. It also led to awful factory working conditions and terrible slums.

The invention of the **silicon** chip means that even the smallest, cheapest handheld device can process a huge amount of information compared to the largest, most expensive computer made before silicon chips. We are really only just beginning to realize how this revolution has affected work and daily life, though. As we have seen, in many ways the chip has made our lives safer, more comfortable, and more entertaining. In other ways it has made our lives less active and more impersonal.

These astronauts from different countries live together in the International Space Station that orbits Earth. Silicon chip technology has made life in space possible, and is helping to break down barriers between nations.

The world in a screen

The television and computer screen have become a window on the world for many people, but there is a price. People who spend hours in front of screens for work and then hours more for leisure spend little time on physical activity and become less healthy as a result.

Silicon chip **technology** has shortened distances and helped to break down national barriers because there is now more communication between different parts of the world. People living thousands of miles apart can work together without ever meeting face to face or going to an office. Business and shopping can be done online. Students can complete college without ever setting foot in a lecture hall.

Thanks to the silicon chip, there is also plenty of entertainment to be had without ever leaving the house. There is concern, however, about what will happen to people who no longer need to get together for work and play. It may be that they lose certain personal skills, or become cut off from real life.

Scientists predict that, within this century, computers will be more "intelligent" than people. Only time will tell how advanced computers can become.

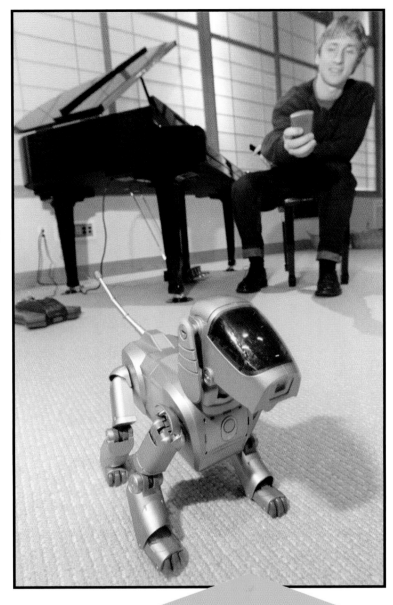

This **electronic** pet dog was shown at a "House of the Future" exhibition in 2000. It is small, remote-controlled, obedient, and clean. **Robot** pets are starting to become a popular alternative to having real animals as pets.

Timeline

1945	First general-purpose **electronic** computer (ENIAC) goes into service
1947	John Bardeen, Walter Brattain, and William Shockley invent the **transistor**
1954	First transistor radios go on sale
1958	Jack Kilby invents the **silicon** chip
1959	Robert Noyce invents the silicon wafer chip
1961	First silicon chips go on sale
1967	Jack Kilby designs one of the first portable calculators
1969	Silicon chips used in the onboard guidance system of Apollo spacecraft
	U.S. Defense Department develops forerunner of the Internet
1971	Intel produces the first **microprocessor**
1972	First commercial video game, "Pong," invented by Nolan Bushnell
1974	First bar code scanner used
1975	Sony produces home videotape system
	First personal computers sold in kit form
1976	Launch of Apple I computer
1977	Launch of Apple II computer
1979	Apple produces the first commercially successful home computer
	Cellular telephones invented
1981	IBM produces a personal computer for office use
1983	First compact discs (CDs) on sale
1985	Windows computer operating system invented by Microsoft
1990	World Wide Web created
1995	**Digital** Video Disc (DVD) invented
	Toy Story, the first film using entirely computer-generated imagery, released

Glossary

amplifier   electronic device that increases the strength of a signal, such as a radio signal

animation   appearance of movement, as in cartoons

appliance   device that performs a task

conductor   substance used to carry electricity

database   collection of information for processing by a computer

digital   coded as numbers

electrical circuit   arrangement of components through which a current can flow

electronic   relating to electrons, the basic particles of electricity, and used to describe devices that operate using electronic power

element   one of about 100 simple substances that make up other substances

germanium   element used for making transistors in the 1950s

guided missile   weapon that travels through the air or water directed by remote control

insulator   substance used to stop the flow of electricity

mass production   manufacture of large numbers of products by machines

microprocessor   main operating parts of a computer when placed on a single silicon chip

modem   device that enables computers to send and receive data through a telephone line

program   to give instructions to a computer or other electronic device by putting in information

revolution   important change in the way things are done

robot   computer-controlled device programmed to do work

satellite   something that goes around the Earth in space

signal   electrical current used to transmit sound or other information

silicon   element used in making electrical circuits

slide rule   measuring device used for making calculations

technology   knowledge and ability that improves ways of doing practical things

transistor   small electronic device that controls the direction of electrical current or acts as an amplifier

vacuum tube   tube from which air has been removed that was used as an amplifier in early electronic devices

valve   device that controls flow of liquid, gas, or electricity through an opening

Further Reading

Casanellas, Antonio. *Great Discoveries and Inventions That Improved Our Daily Lives.* Milwaukee, Wis.: Gareth Stevens, 2000.

Parker, Janice. *Messengers, Morse Code, and Modems: The Science of Communication.* New York, N.Y.: Raintree Steck-Vaughn, 2000.

Sachs, Jessica Snyder. *The Encyclopedia of Inventions.* Danbury, Conn.: Franklin Watts, 2001.

Index